A collection of Bit Programming Interview Questions Solved in C++

Antonio Gulli

Bits is the third of a series of 25 Chapters devoted to algorithms, problem solving, and C++ programming.

DEDICATION

To Leonardo, my second child.
Hoping that you keep your curiosity and energy
for the rest of your life.

ACKNOWLEDGMENTS

Thanks to Antonio Savona for his code review

Contents

1. Given an unsigned int, swap the bits in odd and even positions

Solution

Assume that an unsigned int is 32bits and that we swap the bits in position $2n$ with those in position $2n + 1, n \geq 0$. In order to select all the even bits we can AND with bitmask 0xAAAAAAAAA, which is a 32 bit number with even bits set (0xA is decimal 10, 1010 binary). For selecting all the odd bits we can AND with bitmask 0x55555555, which is a number with all even bits sets (0x5 is decimal5, 0101 in binary). Then we need to shift left (respectively right) of one position and OR the two intermediate results.

Code

```
unsigned int swapBits(unsigned int x)
{
    unsigned int evenBits = x & 0xAAAAAAAA;
    unsigned int oddBits  = x & 0x55555555;

    evenBits >>= 1;
    oddBits <<= 1;
    return (evenBits | oddBits);
}
```

2. Print the binary representation of an unsigned int

Solution

An easy solution is to AND the i_{th} bit with the number 2^i

Code

```
void bin(unsigned n)
{
    for (unsigned int i = 1 << 31; i > 0; i = i >> 1)
    if (n & i) std::cout << 1;
    else std::cout << 0;
}
```

3. Compute whether or not an unsigned number is a power of two

Solution

Suppose that the number is nonzero. If it is a power of two, than the only bit set is in position i. In this case we subtract 1, so all the bits at the left of i will be unset. Therefore a positive number n is a power of 2 if and only if $n \& (n-1)$ is 0. Note that this check only works if $n > 0$

Code

```
bool isPowerOfTwo(unsigned n)
{ return n && (!(n & (n - 1))); }
```

4. Set the i-th bit

Solution

For a given number n we can set the i-th bit with the expression

$$n \mid 1 << i - 1$$

5. Unset the i-th bit

Solution

For a given number n we can unset the i-th bit with the expression

$$n \& \sim(1 << i - 1)$$

6. Toggle the i-th bit

Solution

For a given number n we can toggle the i-th bit with the expression

$$n \wedge (1 << i - 1)$$

7. Given an unsigned number with only one bit set, find the position of this bit

Solution

If there is only one bit set, then the number must be a power of two. For identifying the position set we can AND the number with an appropriate bitmask.

Code

```cpp
unsigned int findPosition(unsigned int n)
{
    unsigned int i = 1, pos = 1;

    while (!(i & n))
    {
        i = i << 1;
        ++pos;
    }
    return pos;
}
```

Solution

Another solution is using the logarithm for returning the position of the only bit set in the given unsigned n. The code returns -1 if n is not a power of 2.

Code

```cpp
int findPosition2(unsigned int n)
{
    if (n & (n - 1))
        return -1;

    return (unsigned int)(log((double)n) / log(2.0)) + 1;
}
```

Solution

Yet another solution runs in $log(log\, n)$. The key intuition is to perform a logarithmic binary search on the log n bits used for representing the unsigned int n.

Code

```
int findPosition3(unsigned int n)
{
    if (n & (n - 1))
        return -1;

    if (n == 1 << 31)
        return 32;

    unsigned int position = 16;
    unsigned int half = 1 << 15;
    unsigned int stride = 16;

    while (1)
    {
        if (n == half)
            return position;
        else if (n > half)
        {
            n = n >> stride;
            position = position + (stride >> 1);
        }
        else
        {
            n = n & ((1 << stride) - 1);
            position = position - (stride >> 1);
        }
        half = half >> (stride >> 1);
        stride >>= 1;
    }

    return position;
}
```

8. Count the number of bits set in an unsigned number

Solution

We can simply loop and count the bits with complexity $O(logn)$, where n is the number of bits in the unsigned.

Code

```cpp
unsigned int countBits(unsigned int n)
{
    unsigned int count = 0;
    while (n)
    {
        count += n & 1;
        n >>= 1;
    }
    return count;
}
```

Solution for sparse bitmaps

This solution works better for sparse unsigned s because it runs in a time proportional to the number of bits set to 1. The line n &= (n − 1) sets the rightmost 1 in the bitmap to 0.

Code

```cpp
unsigned int countBitsSparse(unsigned int n)
{
    unsigned int count = 0;
    while (n)
    {
        count++;
        n &= (n - 1);
    }
    return count;
}
```

Solution for dense bitmaps

This solution works better for dense bitmaps because it runs in a time proportional to the number of bits set to 0. First you must toggle all the bits and then subtract the numbers of the set bits from $sizeof(int)$. The line n &= (n − 1) sets the rightmost 1 in the bitmap to 0.

Code

```
unsigned int countBitsDense(unsigned int n)
{
    unsigned int count = 8 * sizeof(unsigned int);
    n = ~n;
    while (n)
    {
        count--;
        n &= (n - 1);
    }
    return count;
}
```

Solution for 32bit integers

This solution works better for unsigned 32 bits integers. Here you use an additional lookup table containing the number of 1s enclosed in the binary representation of the 8 bit i^{th} number. Using pre-computed lookup tables is a commonly adopted trick for speeding up operations on lookup tables.

Code

```
static int bitInChar[256];

void fillBitsInChar()
{
    for (unsigned int i = 0; i < 256; ++i)
        bitInChar[i] = countBits(i);
}

unsigned int countBitsConstantFor32BitsInt(unsigned int n)
{
    return bitInChar[n & 0xffu] +
        bitInChar[(n >> 8) & 0xffu] +
        bitInChar[(n >> 16) & 0xffu] +
        bitInChar[(n >> 24) & 0xffu];
}
```

9. Add two numbers without using arithmetic operators

Solution

We can use XOR for adding two bits and the AND operator for computing the carry. In the code we also implemented a subtract operation.

Code

```cpp
int add(int x, int y)
{
    while (y != 0)
    {
        int carry = x & y;
        x = x ^ y;
        y = carry << 1;
    }
    return x;
}

int negate(int x) {
    return add(~x, 1);
}

int subtract(int x, int y) {
    return add(x, negate(y));
}
```

10. Given an array of integers where all the numbers are appearing twice find the only number which appears once

Solution

We can identify the only number that appears one time by XOR'ing the array of integers. If a number is duplicate then XOR operation will be 0. In other words, if we XOR all the numbers the result is exactly the number which appears once.

Code

Left as exercise.

11.Given an array of integers where all the numbers are appearing twice find the only two numbers which appears once

Solution

XOR-ing all the numbers produces as result the number $X = n1 \wedge n2$ where $n1$ and $n2$ are the only two numbers which appear once. Let i be the first bit set to 1 in X. We can partition all the numbers into sets: the numbers having the i bit set to 1 and the numbers having it set to 0. Clearly n1 and n2 cannot be in the same set. So the solution of this problem has been reduced to the solution of the previous problem.

Code

Left as exercise.

12.Multiply two numbers without using arithmetic operators

Solution

Without loss of generality let's assume that we multiply x, and $y > 0$. The code is dealing with the case $y < 0$. While $y > 0$ If y is even, we can multiply x by 2 and divide y by 2, otherwise we add x to the result and we subtract 1 to y. The code implements the following logic.

Code

```
int isEven(int n) {
    return !(n & 1);
}

int multiply(int x, int y) {
    int res = 0;
```

```
if (x < 0 && y < 0) {
    return multiply(negate(x), negate(y));
}

if (x >= 0 && y < 0) {
    return multiply(y, x);
}

while (y > 0) {
    if (isEven(y)) {
        x <<= 1 ;
        y >>= 1;
    }
    else {
        res = add(res, x);
        y = add(y, -1);
    }
}

return res;
}
```

13. Compute the two's complement for a given integer

Solution

The two's complement of an n-bit number is the result of subtracting the number from 2^N. The two's complement system has the advantage that the arithmetic operations of addition, subtraction, and multiplication are identical to the ones defined for unsigned binary numbers. This requires inputs to be represented with the same number of bits and any overflow beyond those bits is discarded from the result. Indeed zero has only a single representation.

Code

```
int complement2(int n)
{
    n = ~n;
    n = n + 1;
    return n;
}
```

14.Isolate the rightmost bit set to 1

Solution

Let's build some example. Suppose that $n = 01001100$, if we compute $-n$ in two's complement we get $-n = (10110011) + (00000001) = 10110100$. Therefore $n \& -n$ selects the rightmost bit set to 1.

15. Create a mask for trailing zeros

Solution

If we are able to identify the rightmost bit set to 1, then we can create the mask for trailing zeros just subtracting 1. The solution is therefore $(n \& -n) - 1$

16.Compute parity for a 32 bit number

Solution

Given a number n, we can drop the last bit with the expression $n \& (n - 1)$. Then if the number of bits set to 1 is even, we return 1, otherwise we return 0. In other words, we need to maintain a bit which changes its status from 0 to 1 as many times as the number of bits set to 1 in n. This is achieved in our code with the variable $result$. In many practical implementations we can avoid to process every single bit in isolation by storing a number of pre-computed parity tables for a number of bits.

Code

```
unsigned short parity(unsigned long n)
{
    unsigned short result = 0;
    while (n)
    {
        result ^= 1;
        n &= (n - 1);
    }
    return result;
```

```
}
static int preComputedParity[1 << 16];
unsigned short partityFast(_int64 n)
{
    int mask = 0xffff;
    return preComputedParity[n >> 48] ^
        preComputedParity[(n >> 32) & mask] ^
        preComputedParity[(n >> 16) & mask] ^
        preComputedParity[n  & mask];
}
```

17. Swap two integers variables with no additional memory

Solution

The solution uses XOR operation and it needs no additional storage. The interested reader can think about how to swap two variables which are not integers.

Code

```
void swap(unsigned int & i, unsigned int & j)
{
    i ^= j;
    j ^= i;
    i ^= j;
}
```

18. Swap bit *i* and *j* in a 64 bit number

Solution

If i is equal to j ,no swap is required. We need to swap i and j if those two bits are different, which means that they are XOR'd to 1. If they are different, then there are only two cases possible: (0, 1) and (1, 0) and for those a XOR with 1 will swap the result. If the two bits are different, then their XOR is 0 and for any number $n \wedge 0 = n$. Those observations are implemented in the code below.

Code

```
int swapBits(int n, unsigned int i, unsigned int j)
{
    if (i == j)
        return n;

    int xor = ((n >> i) ^ (n >> j)) & 1;
    return n ^ (xor << i) ^ (xor << j);
}
```

19.Reverse the order of bits in an unsigned integer

Solution

We simply apply the function used for swapping bits. First solution re-use the code defined for a previous exercise, while the second one manipulates bits directly.

Code

```
unsigned int reverse(unsigned int n)
{
    unsigned numBits = sizeof(unsigned int) * 8;
    unsigned halfBits = numBits >> 1;
    for (unsigned int i = 0; i < halfBits; ++i)
        n = swapBits(n, i, numBits - i - 1);
    return n;
}

unsigned int mirror(unsigned int n)
{
    for (unsigned int i = 0; i <= 15; i++)
    {
        n = (n & (0xffffffff - (1 << i) - (1 << (31 - i)))) |
            ((n & (1 << i)) << (31 - i * 2)) |
            ((n & (1 << (31 - i))) >> (31 - i * 2));
    }
    return n;
}
```

20.Convert an integer to a string and a string to an integer

Solution

For a base 10 integer n we know that we can get the last digit with the operation $n \% 10$ and that we can right shift the number with $n/10$. Also the ASCII character for the digit d is $'0' + d$. If the number is negative, we need to prepend character '-'.

Code

```cpp
std::string toString(int n)
{
    if (n == 0) return "0";

    std::string result;
    result.reserve(10);
    if (n<0)
    {
        n = -n;
        result.push_back('-');
    }

    for (int i = log10(n); i >= 0(n); i--)
        result.push_back('0' + (n / (int)pow(10, i)) % 10);

    return result;
}

int toInt(const std::string & s)
{
    if (s.empty()) return 0;

    const bool negative = (s[0] == '-') ? true : false;
    int result = 0;

    for (unsigned int i = (negative ? 1 : 0);
    i < s.size(); ++i)
    {
        if (isdigit(s[i]))
        {
            result = result * 10 + s[i] - '0';
        }
    }
```

```
        return (negative) ? -result : result;
}
```

21.Convert a number from base b1 to base b2

Solution

We can generalize the solution presented in the previous exercise. The idea is to convert from base $b1$ into decimal and from the decimal into base $b2$.

Code

```
std::string convertFromBaseToBase(const std::string & s,
          unsigned int b1, unsigned int b2)
{
    if (s.empty()) return s;

    bool negative = (s[0] == '-');
    int n = 0, reminder;

    for (unsigned int i = (negative ? 1 : 0);
        i < s.size(); ++i)
        n = n * b1 + (isdigit(s[i]) ?
            s[i] - '0' : s[i] - 'A' + 10);

    std::string result;
    while (n)
    {
        reminder = n % b2;
        result.push_back(reminder >= 10 ?
            'A' + reminder - 10 : '0' + reminder);
        n /= b2;
    }

    if (negative)
        result.push_back('-');

    reverse(result.begin(), result.end());

    return result;
}
```

22.Given a set S, compute the powerset of S

Solution

The powerset of S is the set of all the subsets of S. For instance given the set (a, b, c) ,the powerset is
$$((), (a), (b), (c), (a,b), (a, c), (b, c), (a, b, c)).$$
If we represent the presence (absence) of ith element in S with a bit set to 1 (respectively, 0), then we can build the powerset by generating all the bitmasks from 0 to 2^n where n is the size of S. Note that the position of the ith bit is given by $log(i)$.

Code

```cpp
void powerSet(const std::vector<char> & set)
{
    for (unsigned int i = 0; i < (1 << set.size()); ++i)
    {
        unsigned int n = i;
        while (n)
        {
            unsigned int bit = n & ~(n - 1);
            std::cout << set[log2(bit)];
            n &= n - 1;
        }
        std::cout << ",";
    }
}
```

23.Add two decimal strings representing two integers

Solution

The two strings can represent very large integers. The algorithm used for summing the value is the one taught at primary school.

Code

```cpp
int padDecimalStrings(std::string &str1, std::string &str2)
{
    int len1 = str1.size();
    int len2 = str2.size();
```

```cpp
    if (len1 < len2)
    {
        str1.insert(0, len2 - len1, '0');
        return len2;
    }
    else if (len1 > len2)
        str2.insert(0, len1 - len2, '0');

    return len1;
}

std::string addDecimalStrings(std::string s1, std::string s2)
{
    int len = padDecimalStrings(s1, s2);
    int b1, b2, sum, carry = 0;
    std::string res;
    res.resize(len);

    for (int i = len - 1; i >= 0; i--)
    {
        b1 = s1[i] - '0';
        b2 = s2[i] - '0';
        sum = (b1 + b2 + carry);
        carry = sum / 10;
        res[i] = (char)sum % 10 + '0';
    }
    if (carry)
        res = '1' + res;

    return res;
}
```

24. Generate all the bit patterns from 0 to 2^{n-1} such that successive patterns differ by one bit.

Solution

Those patterns are named Gray code after the inventor Frank Gray[1]. It is convenient to generate them incrementally as $(0, 1), (00, 01, 11, 10), (000, 001, 010, 011, 110, 111, 101, 100), (..)$ If we analyze the pattern, we understand that any list L_i is generated from the previous list L_{i-1} in three steps. At the beginning each element in

---

[1] http://en.wikipedia.org/wiki/Gray_code

L_{i-1} is prepended by a 0. Then the list L_{i-1} is reversed and each element is prepended by a 1. As final step the two intermediate lists are juxtaposed to create the new list L_i. This process is repeated until we generate L_{n-1}.

Code

```cpp
void gray(unsigned int n)
{
    if (n == 0)
        return;

    std::vector<std::string> gray;
    gray.push_back("0");
    gray.push_back("1");

    for (int i = 2; i < (1 << n); i = i << 1)
    {
        for (int j = i - 1; j >= 0; j--)
            gray.push_back(gray[j]);
        for (int j = 0; j < i; j++)
            gray[j] = "0" + gray[j];
        for (int j = i; j < 2 * i; j++)
            gray[j] = "1" + gray[j];
    }

    for (unsigned i = 0; i < gray.size(); i++)
        std::cout << gray[i] << std::endl;
}
```

25.Represent unsigned integers with variable length encoding using the continuation bit

Solution

The key idea is to take a 64bit unsigned integer n and represent it with a list of bytes. For each byte seven bits are used for storing the integers with variable length encoding. In addition the most significant bit is the continuation bit and it is used to signal whether or not we need an additional byte for encoding n. For example: if the number is less than 2^7, we need only one byte where the most significant bit it set to 0. Otherwise if the number is less than 2^{13}, we need two bytes where the first byte has the continuation bit set to 1 and the second byte has the continuation bit set to 0. This representation is used for saving space when implementing an inverted index[2], a data structure frequently used by search engines. The inverted index is similar to the analytical index used to memorize the page where a word occurs in a book. The crucial intuition is to store the difference between two consecutive pages for each word and adopt a variable length encoding in order to save space.

Code

```
void encodeContinuationBit(__int64 n,
    std::vector<unsigned short> & encode)
{
    __int64 x = n;
    unsigned short e;
    if (!x) encode.push_back(0);

    while (x)
    {
        e = x & 127;
        x >>= 7;
        if (x)
            e |= (1 << 7);
        encode.push_back(e);
    }
}
```

26. Represent an integer with variable length encoding using gamma encoding

Solution

Gamma encoding is another variable length encoding for integers[3]. The number x is represented with $2\lfloor log_{10}(x)\rfloor + 1$ bits. The integer is separated into two parts. The former is the highest power of 2 not greater than x (say 2^N) and it is represented in unary with log(x) bits set to 0 followed by a 1. The latter is the remaining binary digit representing $x - 2^N$.

---

[2] http://en.wikipedia.org/wiki/Inverted_index
[3] http://nlp.stanford.edu/IR-book/html/htmledition/gamma-codes-1.html

Code

```cpp
void gammaEncoding(unsigned int x)
{
    int i;
    unsigned lenOfX = 0;

    for (i = x; i > 1; i >>= 1) // floor(log2(x))
        lenOfX++;
    for (i = lenOfX; i > 0; --i)
        std::cout << '0';
    std::cout << '1';
    x -= (1 << lenOfX);         // reminder
    for (i = 1 << (lenOfX -1); i > 0; i >>= 1)
    if (x & i)
        std::cout << 1;
    else
        std::cout << 0;
}
```

27. Represent an integer with variable length encoding using delta encoding

Solution

Delta encoding is another variable length encoding for integers[4]. The number x is represented with $\lfloor log_2(x) \rfloor + 2\lfloor log_2(\lfloor log_2(x) \rfloor + 1) \rfloor + 1$ bits. The integer is separated into two parts. The former one is the highest power of 2 not greater than x (say 2^N) and it is represented by encoding the number $N + 1$ with gamma encoding. The latter one is the remaining binary digit representing $x - 2^N$.

Code

```cpp
void deltaEncoding(unsigned int x)
{
    int len = 0, lengthOfLen = 0, i;
    for (int i = x; i > 0; i >>= 1)  // 1+floor(log2(num))
        len++;
    for (int i = len; i > 1; i >>= 1)  // floor(log2(len))
        lengthOfLen++;
```

---

[4] http://nlp.stanford.edu/IR-book/html/htmledition/gamma-codes-1.html

```
    for (int i = lengthOfLen; i > 0; --i)
        std::cout << 0;
    for (int i = lengthOfLen; i >= 0; --i)
        std::cout << ((len >> i) & 1);
    for (int i = len - 2; i >= 0; i--)
        std::cout << ((x >> i) & 1);
}
```

28.Compute the average with no division

Solution

This problem solves a bug in binary search and merge sort reported in 2006 more than 60 years after the first binary search algorithm has been published.[5] Binary search is typically implemented as it follows:

```
int binSearch(int a[], unsigned int size, int key) {
    int low = 0;
    int high = size;
    while (low <= high) {
        int mid = (low + high) / 2;
        int midVal = a[mid];
        if (midVal < key)
            low = mid + 1;
        else if (midVal > key)
            high = mid - 1;
        else
            return mid; // key found
    }
    return -(low + 1);  // key not found.
}
```

and the bug is in the line int $mid = (low + high) / 2;$ since the sum overflow to a negative value if the sum of low and $high$ is greater than the maximum positive int value $(2^{31} - 1)$. In C and C++ this causes an array index out of bounds with unpredictable results. In other languages this situation will throw and exception. The solution is to compute:

$$mid = ((unsigned\ int)low + (unsigned\ int)high)) >> 1$$

---

[5] http://googleresearch.blogspot.co.uk/2006/06/extra-extra-read-all-about-it-nearly.html

It is quite amazing to think that it took more than 60 years to detect a bug in a piece of code so commonly used in the industry and studied by generations of students and academics!!

ABOUT THE AUTHOR

An experienced data mining engineer, passionate about technology and innovation in consumers' space. Interested in search and machine learning on massive dataset with a particular focus on query analysis, suggestions, entities, personalization, freshness and universal ranking. Antonio Gulli has worked in small startups, medium (Ask.com, Tiscali) and large corporations (Microsoft, RELX). His carrier path is about mixing industry with academic experience.

Antonio holds a Master Degree in Computer Science and a Master Degree in Engineering, and a Ph.D. in Computer Science. He founded two startups, one of them was one of the earliest search engine in Europe back in 1998. He filed more than 20 patents in search, machine learning and distributed system. Antonio wrote several books on algorithms and currently he serves as (Senior) Program Committee member in many international conferences. Antonio teaches also computer science and video game programming to hundreds of youngsters on a voluntary basis.

"Nowadays, you must have a great combination of research skills and a just-get-it-done attitude."

www.ingramcontent.com/pod-product-compliance
Lightning Source LLC
Chambersburg PA
CBHW041148050326
40689CB00001B/534